Loved Ones

Loved Ones

Kevin Klein

GREG KOFFORD BOOKS
SALT LAKE CITY

Published in the USA.

ISBN: 978-1-58958-839-4 (paperback)
Also available in ebook.

Greg Kofford Books
P. O. Box 1362
Draper, UT 84020
www.gregkofford.com
facebook.com/gkbooks
twitter.com/gkbooks

Library of Congress Control Number: 2025951329

To Leah, Lexi, and Tyler—my loved ones.

Contents

Introduction

These poems honor people who have taught me faith, hope, charity, and love. You might recognize this list as Paul's essential Christian virtues from 1 Corinthians 13, to which Joseph Smith appended "love" in Doctrine and Covenants 4. Why the addition, when many Bible translations actually use the word "love" in place of the King James "charity"? When even Nephi declares that "charity is love," and Moroni defines charity as "the pure love of Christ"?

Here's a possible answer: our souls grow from feeling this pure love of Christ for ourselves and others, but from what I know about Jesus, he ultimately wants me to feel the pure love of Kevin for them. Writing poetry is for me a form of repentance—not necessarily the guilt-confession-restitution process, but a gratifying divineward expansion of perception and heart—that teaches me charity, which leads me to love. Is love truly the fulfillment of charity? Well, "charitable" describes me, but "lovable" describes my neighbor. I think Brother Joseph was on to something.

May these poems help you develop the faith, hope, and charity sufficient to love the self and the others entrusted to you.

Presentation

There are forty poems in this collection, grouped thematically into ten each about—you guessed it—faith, hope, charity, and love. After each poem there's a QR code to a Substack post with the poem's full text, a video of me reading it, images and links to relevant material and notes about the poem's backstory, influences, and techniques. If these resources help you better appreciate the poems, then the poems have a greater chance of helping you better appreciate your own loved ones.

Invocation

I have been called to cast aside fears,
to live and tell a story.
Called to write the words of a song
and if some of my words fit wrong,
may at least their melody ring
memorably in a few glad ears
for Thy glory.

I. Faith

Sufficiently Instructed

God wipes the soil from his hands
on his robe and points.
"Don't eat that fruit
or you'll die," He says.
Yes, yes, they nod.
Don't eat that fruit.

God squints. "You have no idea
what the hell I'm talking about
will be like if you do, right?
Yes, yes, they nod. *I mean, no.*

God shakes His head.
"What does it mean to be dead?"
His question settles mist-like
in that sterile air until they stare
where their shoes will soon be

and shrug. How could they know
what it means to be apart,
how it feels not to grow?

God sighs. "Well, it's a start.
Off you go." And thus
they become one of us.

An Invitation to the Gospels

We humans are dirt.
Dust of the earth,
worms' meat and dung,
far-flung particles of stars.

Clay breathed upright
and set free to collapse
in our choice of direction,
this life one long sigh.

How did we come to matter?
How could the few words of a lonely man
and his agony of understanding
give humans a destiny to join him
forming worlds and stars without end?

"Now I know that man is nothing," whispers a shocked Moses.
"Nothing less than all my work and glory," God responds.
Did they share a chuckle at this?
If so, it is the laughter
at the heart of the joy
at the heart of the Gospel.

We plant and tend God's word
with faith and obedience.
But where does it grow best?
Humility. From Latin *humus*: soil.
Humor. From Latin *humere*: moisture.
Human. The Proto-Indo-European root for *earth*.

The word, says Alma, needs soil and water in our hearts.
The Word, says John, wants hearts with soil and water,
fertile ground for seeds, and patience
to sprout in his unhurried sunlight.

Some seekers, a few followers worked out
the fear and trembling from salvation
through the playful grace he offered.

Come, delight in their stories.
Nurture your faith and obedience
with humility and a good sense of humor.
Don't be offended by the easiness of the way.
Dust moves hither and thither. Stones obey
or shout hosanna unbidden.

Let his works take root in your heart
and bloom through humility and humor.
Bring forth fruit meet for repentance
and feast with a smile on your face.
He will laugh at the juice down your chin.
Make sure He's laughing with you.

To Christ Crucified

Translation of a seventeenth-century Spanish sonnet,
possibly by Fray Miguel de Guevara

What moves me to adore you, my Lord God?
No promises of heavenly reward
nor fear of hell or judgment's fiery sword
convert your shepherd's crook into a prod—

No, you yourself move me, my spirit awed
at seeing you mocked on the cross, dear Lord;
the mercy for your torturers you implored
to draw our hope and shed your grace abroad.

May this love capture me in such a way
that, heaven fallen, I would still love you
and fear you still with no hell to dismay.

Your gifts do not requite my love as pay;
for if all words between us prove untrue,
through love alone I'd learn again to pray.

Undaunted

After an illustration by Dan Burr

The boy,
always in a billowy white shirt,
brown trousers, and that vest—always
unseasonably clean, mid-stride
across a spring-green field. In the distance
he'll climb the fence of his family's land
and customs, leave this cultivation
for the flaring canopy of ancient trees,
too dense for more than glimpses
of the space they make. He's too young
to sense us watching him, to know how small
the field makes him, how small he will make
this world, one seedling in the wilderness
of a universe he makes a land of promise.

How that old-growth forest becomes a grove
for those who enter empty-handed, always
beyond their pastures, always early sunlight
casting out the dark from shadows.
How the seekers tread home after, dirt caked
on pant legs and smeared across the back
of shirts, always dangling twigs
and last year's leafmeal, one hand
swishing the dew off grass with a stick
and the other cradling their soul, at once
afire with heavenly love and puzzled,
always describing a scatter of acorns
that will become these oaks:
Mother, truth, Presbyterianism.

A Better Country

Hebrews 11:13–16

With seedling splintered bone and seminal tears
they planted furrows of themselves to please
the God of distant rest, whose mysteries
confirmed the city and sustained its seers.
And they confessed their strangeness, pioneers
in wilderness that filled with enemies.
The land tamed them with hunger and disease;
they grew into the vigor of their fears.

Those pilgrim bones shot roots that cracked the rock
of their foundation into useful dirt.
We raise our fortunes where they plowed, possessed
by an inheritance that we must walk
away from for their faith to be preserved:
lugging the promises, leaving behind the rest.

Pioneer Woman, St. George

She brought her family to this god-
forsaken place at His request.
She will petition until He reconsiders
and crops cover the reproach
of a parched red valley where
not a single tree grows.

Only yesterday they unhitched the team,
emptied the wagon, pitched the tent.
Everything they lack is exactly
what they'll ask Him with: is faith.

Tomorrow begins the digging, cutting,
carting water in leaky, too-small buckets
from streams they've already named
and prayed for to run through summer.

All day, heat waves conjured the mirage
or vision of oases, towns, a promised land
that will flourish through His covenants
and hers.
The late sun glares
across a horizon of olive sagebrush.
The woman shields her solemn
brown and green-flecked eyes
from the past, its poverty and riches.
Shields them from this sunset,
squints but doesn't blink
until the bushes flame, until she too
is afire and not consumed.

Lord of Chapel Cleaning

I. Offices

Two forces move the universe:
the push of Simeon's shovel under dung
still steaming from altar-bound bulls,
the pull of Anna's broom through dust
rising afire in slanted morning light.

Each push, each pull stirred up the trail
of cloud the infant God descended;
daily-faithed (how else?) Him finally barnward
before the shepherds, and just in time,
to the patchwork tabernacles of those priestly arms.

They track his hazy eyes and listen. Worship,
the simplest of rhythms, has tuned their souls
to the lift and fall of his music, and they sing
old scripture into prophecy.
                                        Then return,
we imagine, to their offices of praise
and supplication; retire and rise day after day,
lighting lamps and candles in cathedrals
and homes, temple-bereft and cloistered,
chanting vespers polishing chalices dusting stained glass
raking leaves and shoveling snow with hands
whose clockwork ministrations all rehearse
that moment they once held still in his service:
cradling him as the centuries rushed by
in both directions, and when he cried,
rocking him back to sleep. Back and forth,
ticking us toward his millennial embrace,
always through these motions in this place.

II. Offering
Thus their white-haired ritual descendant
comes each Saturday morning to the chapel,
wrangles the stubborn, snorting sacrificial
canister vacuum by the hose, rakes and angles
its mouth between the pews, debris whisked up
in clackety rapture, consuming the crumbs
and pits and husks of communal worship.

The self-closing doors to class and bathroom
croak open, groan closed behind him.
He wears no earbuds. Mind empty of all
but breath, quickening with effort.
What pulses in and out of his heart?
Pure love for God and unadulterated fear
of missing a spot. Of missing his spot. Of not
being missed. They mix in his blood and he exhales
judgment: the Saturday no-shows, the Sunday
chronically late; all those who take more than give,
who give more than he does. He too hears the call
his forebears followed. It is what drives him.

Therefore he pushes the cleaning cart into each room,
pulls half-full trash liners out, fits new ones on,
accepts help if it doesn't replace him.
Praying like his ancestors for Immanuel to come,
yes, for the reign of peace but also to be found
anxiously engaged in the Master's cause—
and He does return, the Lord: suddenly
to this very chapel, just in time to witness
the old man tug inexcusably adult toenail clippings
from the cultural-hall carpet with bare fingers.
Side by side they wipe glass doors, dust painting frames,
silently scrub urinals, mop bathroom tiles.

Jobs finished, Jesus palms the man's bad shoulder:
"Well done, thou good and faithful. Now, please,
stop pushing your sacrifice onto me as payment
or worse, repayment. You can't pull up your soul
any higher than these bootstraps that you've made.
Take them off. Let me wash your feet.
All pushing and pulling that brought me here
has been fulfilled in me. Sufficient is my day
for all to receive me gladly, and give themselves away."

Sabbatical

Between Sunday October General Conference Sessions

A hot fall day, tree shade still inviting,
flames atop only the tallest maples.

The same sunlight that lifts my chin
fed ferns once, then dinosaurs, then
it rested.
                    Rested into oil
and returned as fire through sky
in the airplane's drone that emerges,
as it always does, from the amber
quiet of closed eyes.

Just once, to be nothing
but a part of creation, not always
its fervent purpose, Thy work and glory.
For now, to be no more important
or eternal than this late-morning
chatter of birds.

My soul, let go of salvation,
of principles and ordinances.
Rest from your faith and works.
Lose them all for this moment
so you may find them.

Sunset, West Utah Desert

For Devon
My friend, you wouldn't believe
the sunset across this washboard track
to your favorite wilderness. *Trust me*,
you said, and here I am, and here it is:
yellow sliver of horizon big-bangs
into waves of pink and purple cloud puffs
toasted gold against pale blue that atmosphere
and metaphor bend into heaven, ridged
by the sagebrush-jagged silhouette
of hillside trickling into night.

God painted it all just for me
to offer you. My proof?
You're grinning as you read this,
you who wouldn't laugh at me
even if I tried to persuade you face-to-face
that this personal sunset bit was true,
you whose faith in death yields goodness
that needs no mansions, you who'd rather
damn yourself for loving the world too much
than not enough, you lightning-strike
against the universal dark, you reason
every final curtain is a veil.

And if I meet a closed gate riding westward,
I'll call on saints and angels—but first you,
who'd rush from whatever kingdom you're enjoying
and raise such hell they'll have to let me through.

Backyard, Mid-Winter, With My Eighteen-Year-Old Son

It seems too soon
and feels cruel, I know.
For cherries in June
we cut branches in snow.
His job is to prune.
Your job is to grow.

II. Hope

Easter Triptych

The sunsets over doorposts fade to gloom
as praise and wailing mingle in one song.
Now free to follow God through fire and cloud,
we gaze beyond the serpent-sceptered priest,

who broke and crushed himself in that dark room
and garden, who with bruised heel tread upon
the crown; who shouldered exile for the crowd
condemning him in our redemption feast,

which finished with sunrise breaking from the tomb,
with gnashing teeth and hallelujahs drawn
at once from every mouth unwound of shroud—
we squint, cold faces lightening from the east.

Cradled

Son, if my breath were mine to give.
If I had more than a ragged few
to welcome and say goodbye to you.
If we knew your mother could only live

with this choice. *Go in peace*
I sing, *And He has sent you here*,
then come Himself achingly near.
His hand on my shoulder, I release

you with my blessing and my name.
How, from so slight a father's touch
can I miss you, miss Him, this much?
Was He homesick too when the same

call to save sent His son away?
Hush little baby, and your heart
stops racing, stops. We start
life over: His breath into our clay.

Allergies

for Janet

On Mother's Day it snows
in our backyard, the kind that grows
on cottonwoods and makes my nose
itch inside the nostrils, almost close
but somehow still drip; and as it blows
into the grass (the cotton, that is), I see your clothes
and the pet hair stuck in them—all those
rabbits, ducks, dogs, and cats that I suppose
you never thought about wanting, but chose
for your kids, the way a tree knows
its seeds will fall, and makes pillows
for their landing when the wind throws
them beyond even your branches' shadows.

Into Thy Hands

For parents of children not healed

Lord,
you brought back Lazarus, Lord,
and the widow's son and
Jairus's daughter and Lord

I am uncovering your feet I am
clutching your hem I am
calling out to you despite
being hushed I am
daubing my eyes with mud
and I love your nation I have
built you a synagogue I have
anointed you with tears
with perfumed oil I am poured out
like water pressed like oil I am
asking you to watch one hour with me
and the next and the next and the next please

let this cup pass from me but if not
let me at least sleep for sorrow
till dawn breaks through, and if I wake
still in vapor-thick dark may I wait
in anguish for the sun but if not

I will press the nail prints in your hands I will
commend my spirit into your hands I will
kneel beside as you cry terrified
through all the world's nightmares I will
cry until the angel's breath is on my neck
and your hands upon my head I will
try to believe so desperately my heart
breaks and spills its blood and water I will
believe my wounds are yours my will
is yours, that you will turn to me
from taking me upon yourself and say

thine affliction   *it is finished*   *peace be still*

Middle School Band Concert

We fill the auditorium, abuzz.
The lights dim, a hush falls,
the backing band strikes up
and God strides onstage, beaming.
No need, of course, for a spotlight.

He waves to each of us at the same time
and keeps his pitch to a single slide:
three circles in a row, then three more
stacked, with some arrows between them.
A pause to let it sink in, and oh—
how we morning stars applauded!
Or did the war happen first?
Who knows. Was there even a Q&A?
No one remembers. It seems, though,
that by design we came slowly
and only through unspeakable loss
to any certainties. Birth and death,
sure—but this cosmically important,
comically larval stage—was it really
worth fighting over? At any rate,

here we are: mortality.
The junior high of eternity.
Here we are at our son's first
band concert of 7th grade.
The warmup evokes to closed eyes
a protest of plaintive zoo animals,
their cries for freedom strangled
by the lifting of a baton.
In that mercifully silent unison
we brace ourselves.

There is a slo-mo explosion of tempos
and pitches. There is no other way.
We tap our feet in sympathy,
telepathy, saying *here my dear child is the beat.*
God, in that premortal rally You chose
this as Your hype song, these as Your MCs.
No scale model of our fallen world,
no case studies, disability simulations
or drunk goggles could have prepared us,
which was Your whole point. I watch
a page of sheet music topple off
a tuba player's crooked stand,
and somehow without missing a beat
his tubamate shifts her own
between them with one hand.
It doesn't improve the song.
Just the concert.

For I Will Consider Thy Servant Oliver Granger

(after Christopher Smart & His Cat Jeoffry)

And again, I say unto you, I remember my servant Oliver Granger, behold, verily I say unto him that his name shall be had in sacred remembrance from generation to generation, forever and ever, saith the Lord.
— Doctrine & Covenants 117:12

I love the memory of my father.
— Sarah Granger Kimball, Autobiography
*(*Woman's Exponent*, Sept. 1883)*

For I will consider Thy servant Oliver Granger.
For his name, Thou didst decree through Brother Joseph,
shall be held in sacred remembrance forever.

For some call this a failed revelation.

For if Brigham and the brethren commandoed back
to Far West under death threats and a springtime moon,
laid the temple cornerstone, sang, prayed, and left on missions
from exactly then and there because one year before
Joseph had thus-spoken it, then please, Dear Reader,
like and share this poem for the blessed sake
of prophecy-fulfilling faith and Oliver Granger.

For at thirty-three he went mostly blind due to "exposure."
For in the absence of more detailed primary sources,
Google says his corneas might have frozen.
For he became a licensed Methodist exhorter and exhorted away
in a licensed manner until he met the Mormons and their book.
For Moroni appeared to him one night, said kneel
and told him what to pray for. Also mentioned preaching.

For Oliver served two missions and baptized the Wilsons
of later Wilson Lane fame in Ogden, Utah. For Oliver earned
no place-names himself, the town of Granger so called
for its rich soil, not his good works in redeeming

the bad deeds of that best-intentioned Zion.
For when Marks and Whitney couldn't quite forsake
the Kirtland kingdom, Oliver went commanded back
to fall and rise again, failing gloriously in a lost cause,
contending for the Presidency's debt and property,
squinting at paperwork he sanctified with an integrity
the gentile creditors commended. For if anyone
has reason to peace-out of the Church for finances
it was he, sole shoveler-after-upper for the scant
balance of his forty-seven planetary years.
For Church History sources in which his name appears
are mostly conveyances and affidavits.

For over his only plot of land, a tombstone
stands weatherworn in Kirtland since 1841.
For it reads OLIVER GRANGE, a tiny R
wedged in at the end, some stone carver's
shortsighted work. For Lord, Thou and Oliver
still laugh about it when ye see each other
in paradise, still invite all litigants of defaulted oracles
to open culture-blinded eyes: Oliver's name
indeed lives on in sacred remembrance
through his daughter, Sarah Granger Kimball.
Boss lady of this dispensation, woman's rights woman,
speaker, listener, leader in the cause for Zion,
herself a cause of Zion. Presiding in the visionary present,
she built Relief Society in swamp and desert
with wisdom, sisterhood, and priestly powerful hands.

For her tombstone reads "Strong-Minded and Warm-Hearted."
For in her and all such consecrated women
of song- and speech- and statue-worthy labors,
men cannot hope for any greater honor
bestowed in heaven's earthly queen-and-kingdom
than to be called their father.

With Those That Mourn

Jesus wept, says John,
but not why. How he loved him,
they said, but not how
love kept him away four days
beyond the soothing voices
then the wailing and despair.
Lord, if thou hadst been there…

When comforters go home,
once cards and flowers dry up
the ache becomes a tomb you must
remain in, and no one's words
can call you forth before your time—

So we cry in greeting and farewell
as you emerge, still wrapped in cloth,
wincing at sunlight, stumbling down
a path we can't follow, but embrace you
and embrace again, if only to delay
your over-the-shoulder nod
and wave of a bandaged hand.

Children

for Lindsay and Kyle

For you, child, who came
cold into the world, we invite
a village of kindred migrant souls
to this winter mountainside
in your honor, if not memory, tonight.

They too have held hands
and watched helpless, have risen
in shock before dawn and left
footprints like these in the snow
from homes they will never go back to.

They sing and pray with us and keep
your brothers from the propane heater
and stand still as we cry on their shoulders,
as the stars descend into sight.

To raise you, child, we light
candles inside paper lanterns,
hold them steady as our warmth
becomes your glow.
Then we let go.

The Making of a Patriarch

for Dave Black, a good man and survivor of the following true story

My life should have ended
on that altar of ice and stone
when I fell, or rapidly descended
sixty feet beside the frozen waterfall
that I'd been climbing ropeless and alone.

That's all. My life should have ended
and it did; it was no longer mine.
I plummeted, slid feet-first, blew out my spine,
but several natural laws had been suspended
for that and some cracked ribs to be the worst.
I wasn't paralyzed, no organs burst
or cleanly broken bones. I couldn't walk,
but at least I wouldn't bleed to death alone
and hopeless. In my parka was the phone
that I'd reactivated the day before,
and I could breathe in just enough to talk.

If I'd been made an angel, who could tell
the messenger from message that I bore?
After having rapidly descended, or plain fell
through that December dusk, with no blood spilled
outside my skin, and nothing broken but my heart
at how these wings' white feathers filled
the ambulance from my parka ripped apart
by an EMT to save my life when clearly
it was not in danger and no longer mine—

why did I make that ropeless, lonely climb?
My family and I myself have dearly
wanted to know. Who understands?
A martyr's gamble to flush out the face
of God, or find the only place
that's safe from Him: His hands.

And here I am, an angel who descended
or plain fell—what matters is the mark
of my belonging: steel rods in my back.
One for Moses, one for Aaron, both
to turn my forty Sinai years to growth.
Whatever I become or have or lack,
there's no deciding now. I hear
His thoughts in mine, a whisper not to fear
the kindly light more faithfully than the dark.
Climbing once more, roped and not alone,
lifting the trust of children with my own,
a fallen angel, rising patriarch.

Summer Mountainside Wedding, Second Time Each

We finally have lost all hope for you,
delighted as we are to lay it down
in favor of contentment with this new
match made for heaven, but on common ground

reclaimed from burning, and by flames prepared
to plant yourselves and tend each other. Here
in this insistent garden you have shared
your labor's fruits with grace-gifts that appear

each spring: these buried seeds that will survive
to blaze with flowers after snow and drought.
Sometimes we can't do any worse than thrive.
Sometimes ultimately everything works out:

even the smoke from wildfires drifting over
serves your pictures as perfect cloud cover.

III. Charity

Twelve Ways of Taking the Sacrament

1.
Bless and sanctify this bread
to the souls of all those who partake
and especially those few who instead
stare down and with one shake
of a chin-resting-in-the-palm head
send the tray past them, or take
only the handle and lean across the spread
of bench to the old couple half-awake,
the woman who looks up startled, eyes red,
unfolds herself, and smiles all our heartache.

2.
The priest for the water prayer kneels,
gray-blond ponytail-tight scalp
hovering just above the tray-cloth.
Still wet behind the ears from baptism
last week, he clears his raspy throat
for courage. Years of drinking, drunk
more often than not, face more texture
than complexion, crumpled newspaper section
of local tragedies that no clean living
or priesthood blessings will smooth out
in this lifetime, and with a voice
that won't fully scab over, asks God
to bless and sanctify this water.

This water, he repeats, swallowing audibly,
stumbling through that winding sentence
of blunt words, nerves and joy shaken
and stirred. When the trays return
he reaches down, lifts up, and stops.
Not the first time he's measured
his worth in the bottom of a cup.

Then, face unscrunching into something
like a grin, he raises his hand as if to toast
the One who bought this round for everybody,
each round for all eternity, whose grace
is an open tab—and quick as forgiveness
knocks back that holy thimble like a shotglass.

3

I know I should have my eyes closed, but it's hard not to watch Sister Taylor bless the sacrament each Sunday. When the priest kneels down she stands up on the other side of the chapel, in front of the first row where her husband, their kids James and Jasmine, and Brother and Sister Alvarez, who are deaf too, all sit. She stays right on pace with the priest, her mouth and eyebrows moving almost as much as her hands. I'm beginning to understand some sign language just by watching her. Maybe I'll take it in high school. That means *Father*, that means *souls*, and sometimes she dabs her eyes, a quick tap in each corner with one finger of the same hand. Maybe she's crying, but it could be part of the sign for Jesus. Of her sign for Jesus.

4

Joseph was right about the sacramental wine:
beware of any faith you haven't made yourself.
Here are grapes and bottles. Here is time.
Here is sabbath after sabbath for your cellar shelf.

5

I ease the cup out,
drink, discard, and witness
a water bubble domed
over its tray-hole.
Buoyant shiny O
of supplication,
invocation
mourning
invitation
rejoicing: the O
in the center

of hope.

6
The new priest repeats:
"That they may eat it in—"
no there's no ***it*** *I know*
it seems like there should be
and what difference does it make
if eating the bread specifically
or just the act of eating
is done in remembrance or is
the lack of it just to keep
us careful when we read it,
and he says it again, eat it
in remembrance and on
the third time I hear it:

the body of Thy Son
the body of Thy Son
the body of Thy Son

7
Can you imagine:
Come to my arms, ye blessed.
Right now, dust filaments
twirling slowly, twinkling
in early sunlight through tall
glowing curtains, embracing
their weightlessness, drifting
everywhere but down:
yes I can.

8
Bread tray glinting with reverent
fluorescence, the deacon offers Christ's body
to the body of Christ, row by row,
one by one, then heads out to the foyer,
gathering in:

teens on phones, parents with toddlers,
the man who wears no tie and prefers
a comfy armchair to the pews.
All have eaten and are filled.
Turning back for the chapel
the boy glances outside.
Brother and Sister Larson
totter arm in arm, inch by inch
toward the doors.

By now, the boy knows,
the other deacons are lined up
inside, waiting. The whole ward
is waiting for the priests, who wait
for the deacons, who wait for him,
who waits for the Larsons,
who have waited on the Lord
arm in arm in health and sorrow
through two daughters lost in childhood
and a grandson by suicide last November,
cancer and remission twice, then three missions
in sixty-seven married years.

Four months from yesterday
is Brother Larson's funeral.
Of course the boy doesn't know
this or what to do right now,
but his instinct is to bless.
He pushes through those doors
into a flood of summer, sunlight
flashing off his outstretched tray
like Ephraim's horn, gathering in.

9
The Word made flesh
made bread, soft white
sandwich loaf we suction
and pry out of molar-pits
with tongues, or in extreme
cases, a discreet fingernail,
working with the persistence,
the precision, the relief
of repentance.

10
Without an official component of ritual drama in our sacrament ordinance, I have adopted the weekly struggle between this little girl and her parents. Toddler-tufted in a functional pink dress, she prances and ambles down the aisle, almost losing her balance every fourth step yet still managing to elude their crouched-down-shuffle and furtive swiping for her arm. Those of us with grownup kids revel in the scene, but I understand her parents' reaction. There's the fear of our annoyance and judgment, and perhaps a deeper worry that their daughter is not destroying reverence but fulfilling it. She must be stopped before her joy infects our penitence, before we start wondering if all sacrament hymns have to sound funereal. Before she catches us watching her, stops twirling, and gazes back in radiant amusement as if to ask: *O you who are redeemed, here to celebrate your redemption: why aren't you dancing too?*

11
Three pews ahead,
pudgy hands whack
and grip the bench back.
A wispy noggin rises,
all wobble but the eyes.

They fix me with the gaze of God.
I grin, frown, furrow, gape,
a jack-in-the-box of expressions
and...*pop*! The baby's face breaks
into delight, eyes and mouth
wide with silent cackling.

Now I too can't help but smile:
pride, this flex of dad skills
or simply the thrill of connection,
of communion. She is teetering with joy,
would have toppled over
if not for her vigilant mom.
And because I should be thinking
about Jesus right now,
I bow my head and pray
that every once in a while
and for no good reason
He looks back at me this way.

12
Christmas Day sacrament meeting:
mid-ordinance, the traditional
mewl and wail of babies
in a whole new light,
the original
light.

How to Pray

I pray like they tell me to, like God's in the room. But the room is this palatial open-plan dining area during a party at some tech bro's McMansion. Keeping one eye on Him—God, not the rich guy—I smile and agree as other guests talk at me, shifting around the room so I can stay just close enough to hear what people say to Him:

"Yeah, my back hurts. It really hurts. Right here. Feel that? Push with your finger right here. Can you feel it? Yeah. Right there."

"Why does this *always* happen to *our* family? Why can't we have a *normal* Christmas for once?"

"Oh thank you just so much for everything!"

With my conversation starters ready—"So, was Job based on a real person?" and "How's King David doing these days?"—I make for the appetizers when He does, keeping an item or two behind as we build our plates. I try to count myself in—"Okay: one, two, three, *Excuse me, God . . .*"—but each scoop and tong-drop builds in me the terror of having nothing more to merit His attention with than my existence. Clever questions and sense of timing gone, panic rising that my window of opportunity has closed or was just a mirror to begin with, I remark in His direction, "Boy, that shrimp looks good." But right when I say it someone guffaws across the room, and if He heard me He's not letting on, omniscience and all. So I take the same last few snacks He does, hoping He'll notice and break the ice.

My Angel Mother

Through all the pain and lies I dealt,
the faith and promises unkept,
each night my angel mother knelt
in gentle-spoken prayer and wept.

Yet still how willfully I fell
and cast my covenants aside!
So with her halo she smote the hell
out of me 'til I was sanctified.

Of governing angels, duly tasked
to correlate her methods more,
my angel mother sweetly asked,
"What else did you give me a halo for?"

Believers

I. Atheists
Secretly, deep down,
all the great atheists believe
that secretly, deep down,
God is proud of them

for trying to save the world
from oppression and
even worse, ignorance,
which is exactly what He would do
in their own irrefutable shoes.

II. Fundamentalists
The harvest is past.
We are all gathered in
this ark of a bunker
beneath a dry field.

The world's laughter thins,
tares bristling in the wind.
Their hoarse prophets fade
like cicadas at dusk.

Through me, God's thunder
of judgment is over.
From now on it's lightning
stretched forth like my hand.

You swore no more flood,
so Lord, I pray Thee:
Don't burn the whole world.

Here am I. Allow me.

President Young Welcomes Them into Heaven

And he shall bow down, this modern Moses,
down low to the Egyptians, this
Lion of the Lord, stout graybeard
nursing-father king, shall lick up dust
from feet until they gleam
darker than before. He shall weep
for their unwitnessed beauty
in the Zion he foresaw,

for the mud and straw they have trodden,
for skin cracked raw, whip-scarred
and sold to build a kingdom without hands.
He will wash and heal those feet
with tears, will dry them
with the salt-and-pepper hairs
of his sainted head.

Provo Temple Farewell

Closed for demolition March 1st, 2024

When this world has fulfilled its purpose,
run a victory lap around the sun
and spun one final daytime into night,
sending the last full moon over mountains
like a dove that shall never return
before earth rolls up and burns—
before this luminous intelligence
is released with a vote of thanks,
the gods who grew up here gather
for one more walk through its palaces
and slums, the seashores and gardens
where they harvested memory,
noses and toes awash again
in the grime and grist of awakening.

And even deified, they learn
how different this world smells
from all the others they're making,
like the moment you stepped inside
your house just after the mission,
breathed in and for the first time named
the bread and fabric softener scent of home.

Walking backwards, holding hands,
with tears they believed that eons of divinity
would finally give them dominion over,
they watch the pulling out of stakes,
that grand old firmament collapse
in flood and fire, in ashes and then silence.
A smudge of dust where once the blue marble hung:
the dirt that birthed them waiting their command.

A Blessing on the Food

Fork poised above my bowl of Costco
perfection-in-a-bag kale salad,
I fold my arms and bow my head and stare—
when lo, my eyes themselves turn instruments of prayer:

Lord, the Zion of colors I'm please-blessing!
Mint-white center of brussels sprouts
cross-sectioned, verdant at the crown;
dark, undulating canopy of kale
on tough pale stalks my grateful teeth strip clean.
Cool spears whittled from cores of broccoli trunks,
angelic cabbage wings, a scattering
of solemnly olive pumpkin seeds,
and governing all, the burgundy
chickory flakes and cranberries.
A sociality greater than the sum
of its ingredients, eternal glory
bound in speckled pearlescent
fellowship of poppyseed dressing.

How can I fail to praise these hues, the shades
of hands that brought them in communion here?
The hands that pick, slice, cut, and fix
the tools that pick, slice, cut; those hands
that set and move and set irrigation lines,
that wrench and clean the machinery
and clench and wring at the heavens
over weather, workers, buyers, insects, fate—
for this glad bowl of gathering, may they be
forever nourished and strengthened, Lord:
the hands that have prepared it.

New Deacon

It is our son's first trip down the chapel aisle
steering a silver tray of broken bread.
Repentant faces lift his way and smile:

our flock, dear villagers who raised this child
to bear their burdens, keep their spirits fed
beginning with this trip down the chapel aisle.

He follows solemnly the loping file
of taller boys, and his too-inclined head
makes us turn to each other, shrug, and smile.

This earnestness, and shoes that for a while
will still be much too big, seem to have led
to his hopefully only trip down the chapel aisle:

with scuff, then cry and clatter, clang and sprawl,
the ordinance's dignity has fled.
Startled faces crane his way, then smile

at us. We nod. What better place to fall
than here, where all things rise? Hands rugburn-red,
he picks tray, bread, and self up from the aisle,
too sheepish and too shepherded not to smile.

Last Primary Presentation

We two alone will sing like birds in the cage…
When thou dost ask me blessing, I'll kneel down
And ask of thee forgiveness.

— King Lear

When you dream, there's a chance you'll find
A little laughter, or happy ever after.
—*"You Are the Music in Me,"* High School Musical 2

The song leader lifts her palms.
Children leap from onstage seats.
The gentle piano starts.

Her eyebrows arch, mouth rounds,
arms wave at the elbows, and thin voices rise,
their unison a darting cloud of sparrows.

These children, mumbling through verses
then shouting the choruses, step-stooling
and mouth-breathing their parts
into the podium microphone, yawns
and forgotten lines restored
by whispering teachers, and always
one kid staring into space and another
twirling in place: we chuckle in recognition,
in relief that heaven is evidently not
an eternity of piano recitals,
each piece perfect, worlds without end.

We imagine God smiling too,
but look closer at His face.
Those lines aren't all from laughter.
Children on a small stage, row after row
of grownups between them and the exits:
it's easy here and now to forget
the price He pays for growth. Look closer
at the back line of eleven-year-olds.
This hasn't been their show for years.
They loom behind the smaller kids
like tombstones of childhood,
scarecrows at the field-edge of life.
Never again will their off-script antics
amuse this perpetual audience.

My dear eleven-year-old daughter: it's okay
if you don't sing. I guess I need to hear that
for myself. You and I never could quite heave
our hearts into our mouths, and I forgive you
for not once entertaining us in any Primary program
except when, mortified at your little brother
singing his heart out, you hissed and pinched
until he squealed "Ow, Lexi!" even louder
than he sang, and the whole ward laughed—

Still, like that old king I'm terrified to anger
of you feeling, of me holding, nothing.

The song leader, eyes glistening,
lowers her hands for the last time.
Thus begins a season of goodbyes.
I feel it in the space between my arms:
my chest your first cradle, then foundation
and now launchpad. Not rejection but trust,
I remind myself—this pushing me away
just the stretching of wings.

The kids all jostle down stage steps
except for you. A few gangly flaps
and there you go, above my lap, beyond
our bench, not with the orchestral swell
of a Disney teen musical's final number,
but the postlude "Teach Me to Walk in the Light."

Fly on, dear daughter, past this first
of many sunsets, into the dark
we've always feared and known
it was for this you came to us
with more than eyes and wings.
Fly on, and when your arms
begin to ache, you may find them
beating in time to these old Primary songs,
rising here and there in spiral currents.

They were made to carry you.
I believe in the home they speak of.
Dear daughter, there are many perches
and always only one nest,
where I see myself now waiting,
but in truth am still on my way,
and whose tunes I think I hear
but in truth may just be remembering
because, in those first of our lyrics,
you are the music in me.

If the Savior Stood Beside You

"Every child needs at least one adult who is irrationally crazy about him or her."

— *Urie Bronfenbrenner*

I'll come as a thief in the night, he said,*
turned away from us and hunched over.
Then whirled back, eyes darting,
hands curled into claws.
Took two sneaky steps on tiptoe,
and we laughed.

So when I suddenly stand beside you,
he added, grin fading, gaze lowered, please
don't try to look busy. Accept my gift
of getting over yourselves and greet *me*:
this face you always manage to brighten.
These arms your fear keeps outstretched.

When I stand beside you, I pray
your first thought's the same as mine:
I've missed you so much! Believe me.

Believe me, we'll fix
whatever needs fixing
after I get my hug.

* *Jesus himself didn't actually say this in the New Testament. The day of the Lord is described as coming as a thief in the night by both Peter and Paul, and in Revelation 16:15 the angel speaking on behalf of the Lord says "I come as a thief."*

IV. Love

Fingernails

I reach into the crib on tiptoe, holding
my breath from the railing in my ribs,
angling the headlamp beam from her face
so it doesn't make her squirm or look
impersonally angelic. She is the messenger
of herself, has come in tiny glory to announce
she will not keep her hands still when awake.

There is the tick of the wall clock,
her little breathing, and the click
of my clippers. She has come to make mystical
and fulfilling as religion these tasks of human
housekeeping. In the halo's yellow edge
a frown puckers her face. She stretches, farts,
and turns to let me reach her other hand.

Soft

A drive for its own sake
five o'clock on New Year's Day,
our kids, aged two and one, coming down
from the cocktail of cousins and sugar.

Car-seat straps sink into puffy coats.
Babble and rattling blend
with our parental murmurs,
with hum of road and engine.
Warmth old as the birth of stars,
as old as breath, melts
the crystals of window-frost.

The glow of afternoon fading into dark,
peace as tenuous as a little kid's nap.
The world comes unwrapped
in a tin box. Nothing here is new,
nothing new is needed. It's unsettling
this day and age to feel so complete.

The children might remember
if the womb was any better,
but there's no use asking.
As we slow for a stop sign I turn
to see their sleep-closed faces
in streetlights that glide over them
quiet as snowflakes.

I whisper to my wife. She nods. The silence
becomes our silence. With it we stir
this softness like swizzle sticks
through hot-chocolate froth
that will close over
in its own gentle time.

Sometimes Prayer

For Carol Lynn Pearson

Mom and Dad's door is open.
From the hall I see them in bed,
sitting up, faces flickering glory
and screenlight. Without a glance
away, they scoot a space
between themselves
to nestle me,
and we watch TV.

Youth Soccer Psalm

How precious also are thy thoughts unto me, O God!
— *Psalm 139:17*

O God, though my heart may wander
far from Thee among these oceans
of bumpy grass and their dandelion islands,
these billowing jerseys that prance and clump
around the ball, tumble and sprawl—

though I am one of those kids transfixed
by cheers from other fields and droning planes
through the eternal Saturday morning sky
of this, the rec-league soccer game of life—

Yet Thou knowest my downsitting
when I'm goalie and the ball is far away,
mine uprising to be first in line
for halftime snacks. Thou art acquainted
with all my ways, curiously wrought
as I am, fearfully and wonderfully made
yet a disaster on the field, and yet I know
Thou couldst not think in Thine heart
to kick me off this team, or even bench me
for more than ten minutes. Thou watchest
as I run toward the ball more often than away;
kick it sometimes really far, and usually
in the right direction. And every time
I seek and find Thy face among the parents
who stare into their phones or scream *run*
get that ball push him back ya gotta want it
ya gotta fix my childhood slay your enemies
hate them that fight against you
with perfect hatred—Thou art smiling,
waiting for me to wave
so Thou canst wave back.

Baggage Declaration

To Leah each Valentine's Day

When I say I love you, who
knows better what I mean than you
and St. Valentine himself, third-century
Roman priest whom Emperor Gaius
liked—admired, even—but imprisoned
for trying to convert him: Valentine,
who healed the jailor's daughter
of her blindness, then closed his eyes
and cell, head bowed, hands folded,
refusing to renounce, awaiting
the emperor's roulette of a mind
to land on a sentence? Valentine,
who knew the peace in such uncertainty,
the dread in such love that leads us willingly
into the prisons of ourselves, where we choose
death over walking free, and rise
new creatures, worthier of each other
and this saint whom legend says
sank calmly beneath the blunt clubs
and was beheaded for good measure:
Valentine, who outgrew an empire
that bred its power from fear
by feeding his fear to the power
I feel when I say I love you.

Eternaversary

I knew I'd married a goddess
when she made time stand still
for a plate of pasta salad.
We sat on a blanket in the park.
Green deepened, blue darkened,
sunset bloomed. Mouth full, I asked
about the oil change tomorrow.
Mouth full, chewing with eyes closed,
she raised a finger. Birds hushed.
Trees held their breath. Children
froze mid-swing. *Hold on,* she said.
I'm eating the perfect bite.

It was true. Her fork had pecked and pinned
three pasta spirals and a cube of cheddar
with equal bits of sun-dried tomato
and artichoke, but no olive slices—evidently
goddesses don't have to like olives—
while those of us who do just lowered our eyes
to the paper plate in our lap, dressing-streaks
from this salad we ate without tasting.

I knew then why she mixes words,
forgets names. Does a goddess, who welcomes
atoms and cells into matter and selves
have to read the instructions? Watch her work,
then realize you've joined in her laughter
and dancing like no one is watching
because it's true: they're all dancing too,
singing along to songs whose lyrics
she can't help but get wrong.
No, goddesses don't grant entrance into heaven.
They reach out tree-branch arms and make
heaven in perpetual embrace, they hold us
in the now, the only always now,
perfectly present, breathing, chewing
slowly as eternity—eyes closed,
words working themselves out of meaning.

Thanksgiving Webcam, 2003

So this is the distance it takes between
family to keep us connected. On a screen
at each end of ten thousand miles,
two thumb-sized windows blink awake
and there we are, faces lurching into smiles.
Laughing, we shout each other's names,
watch our own hands wave, and make
crazy faces. Our images slide into the places
where our bodies move, voices hiss
with digital static. Untethered astronaut
too far removed, too in-survival-mode to miss
anyone not in front of me till now, I caught
a glimpse, behind my sister's head,
of hands-in-pocket torsos: my brothers-in-law
and little brother, waiting their turn. I've never said
I wish I was there with you! on the phone
before, but their lining up tugged me across:
That's right where I'd be standing now.
That space we keep for love that feels like loss,
the distance that it takes to have a home.

Bee Mine

To Leah – Christmas 2022

Of all life on earth, only humans
imagine all life on earth
as themselves. No beehive's
been found adorned with paintings
of cute bee-like humans
in attitudes of industrious devotion.

This postcard of a portly male drone
pulling down a heart-flower
for his beloved beneath a pearl-rose
moon in daylight—this utterly
non-evolutionary gesture
has caught his companion by surprise.
There's no nectar in there,
I hear her say. *He knows that, right?*

She hesitates between flying off
for some more promising flower patch
or partner and searching through all her instincts
for how to accept this offering. "Delicious,"
she buzzes, probiscis making the fake slurps
of children at a tea party. "You're amazing,"
she waggle-dances, legs bedazzled
with silver-gold glitter for pollen. "What
would I ever do without you?"

Your Hair

Your hair, my love, is soft and black
with gleaming brown streaks and gray gobs
that drip down my arm from the clot
I pulled out of the bathroom sink trap
with my bare hand because it's your hair.

Consecration

One summer I wrote my poetry under the shade
of our apple tree. My muses were the birds,
who chimed with admirable diligence but made
no useful observations, and lone words

that hummed like bees above me in pursuit
of their own purposes, crossing with mine.
And, sure as blossoms wither into fruit,
I pruned each bloom of sentences into a line.

Then watched success make victims of them both:
bird-pecked, worm-burrowed, page inked up enough
to blight a heart so wholly set on growth—
yet love consists of our attempts to love.

I didn't harvest a single apple or poem.
Paper and pen exchanged for leaves and rake,
I worked for the pride of working for my home
and love of the task at hand for the hand's own sake,

treading lumps I'd hoped would gladden me,
now smeared beneath the limbs they'd fallen from:
returning to the soil that feeds the tree
that bore them, that they never will become.

Benediction

Bless us, Heavenly Father, to return
home safely, but not so much we learn
only to be good children, and please supply
more verbs for our daily lessons than *apply*.

Acknowledgments

Many thanks to J. S. Absher, Christopher John Bissett, D. A. Cooper, Scott Hales, Luke Richards, Ethan Unklesbay, and Darlene Young for their insightful suggestions for these poems. Also, much appreciation for the saintly poets at the MoPoWriMo and MoPoLounge Facebook groups and their downright ministerial fellowship and encouragement.

Previously Published

The Pioneer Woman, St. George: *Dialogue: A Journal of Mormon Thought* 51, no. 3 (2018)

Cradled: *BYU Studies* 61, no. 1 (2022)

New Deacon: *BYU Studies* 61, no. 2 (2022)

Soft: *Dialogue: A Journal of Mormon Thought* 51, no. 2 (2018)

A Better Country: *Dialogue: A Journal of Mormon Thought* 51, no. 2 (2018)

Allergies: *Dialogue: A Journal of Mormon Thought* 57, no. 4 (2025)

Thanksgiving Webcam, 2003: *Irreantum* 18, no. 2 (2022)

Also available from

GREG KOFFORD BOOKS

Re-reading Job: Understanding the Ancient World's Greatest Poem

Michael Austin

Paperback, ISBN: 978-1-58958-667-3
Hardcover, ISBN: 978-1-58958-668-0

Job is perhaps the most difficult to understand of all books in the Bible. While a cursory reading of the text seems to relay a simple story of a righteous man whose love for God was tested through life's most difficult of challenges and rewarded for his faith through those trials, a closer reading of Job presents something far more complex and challenging. The majority of the text is a work of poetry that authors and artists through the centuries have recognized as being one of--if not the--greatest poem of the ancient world.

In *Re-reading Job: Understanding the Ancient World's Greatest Poem,* author Michael Austin shows how most readers have largely misunderstood this important work of scripture and provides insights that enable us to re-read Job in a drastically new way. In doing so, he shows that the story of Job is far more than that simple story of faith, trials, and blessings that we have all come to know, but is instead a subversive and complex work of scripture meant to inspire readers to rethink all that they thought they knew about God.

Praise for *Re-reading Job*:

"In this remarkable book, Michael Austin employs his considerable skills as a commentator to shed light on the most challenging text in the entire Hebrew Bible. Without question, readers will gain a deeper appreciation for this extraordinary ancient work through Austin's learned analysis. Rereading Job signifies that Latter-day Saints are entering a new age of mature biblical scholarship. It is an exciting time, and a thrilling work." — David Bokovoy, author, *Authoring the Old Testament*

Elias—An Epic of the Ages: A Critical Edition

Orson Ferguson Whitney
edited by Reid L. Neilson

Paperback, ISBN: 978-1-58958-828-8

Orson F. Whitney's *Elias—An Epic of the Ages* stands as Mormonism's most ambitious literary achievement, a sweeping poetic retelling of the plan of salvation and the Restoration. First published in 1904 and refined in Whitney's 1914 edition, the ten-canto epic draws upon scripture, history, and inspired imagination to place the life and mission of Jesus Christ at the center of a cosmic narrative that spans premortality, the Savior's mortal ministry, the apostasy, and the dispensation of the fulness of times. In the tradition of Milton's *Paradise Lost* and Dante's *Divine Comedy*, Whitney sought to give his faith a literary monument equal to its spiritual grandeur—an epic in which doctrine, history, and prophecy meet in verse.

This new critical edition, edited by Reid L. Neilson, presents the definitive text of Whitney's 1914 revision alongside rich historical context, literary analysis, and contemporary responses that situate Elias in the cultural and religious landscape of turn-of-the-century Mormonism. Both a devotional masterpiece and a literary artifact, *Elias—An Epic of the Ages* invites modern readers to encounter Whitney's soaring vision anew.

Praise for *Elias—An Epic of the Ages*:

"Orson Whitney was the preeminent Latter-day Saint man of letters at the turn of the twentieth century. Reid Nielson has brought this ambitious writer and poet back to life with a critical edition of Whitney's vast poem *Elias—An Epic of the Ages*. Whitney sought to pour everything he knew and experienced as a gospel believer into one grand work. Neilson annotates *Elias* and embeds it in the sources emanating from Whitney's work: autobiographical reflections, contemporary reviews, Whitney's own critical work, and assessments of Whitney's overall achievement. Anyone interested in Latter-day Saint literature will want this book on their shelves." — Richard Lyman Bushman, author of *Joseph Smith: Rough Stone Rolling*

Boadicea; the Mormon Wife: Life Scenes in Utah

By Alfreda Eva Bell
Edited and Annotated by
Michael Austin and Ardis E. Parshall

Paperback, ISBN: 978-1-58958-566-9

First published in 1855, *Boadicea; the Mormon Wife* belongs to a sub-genre of crime fiction that flourished in the Eastern United States during the 1850s. *Boadicea* has become increasingly important to scholars of Mormonism because it gives us a glimpse of the Mormon image in literature immediately after the Church's public acknowledgement of plural marriage. Over the next half century, this image would be sharpened and refined by writers with different rhetorical goals: to end polygamy, to attack Mormon theology, or just to tell a highly entertaining adventure story. In Boadicea, though, we see these tropes in their infancy, through a prolific author working at break-neck speed to imagine the lives of a strange people for readers willing to pay the "extremely low price of 15 cents" for the privilege of being amazed by stories of polygyny and polyandry, along with generous helpings of adultery, seduction, kidnapping, and no fewer than fourteen untimely but spectacular deaths: people are shot, stabbed, bludgeoned, poisoned, hanged, strangled, and drowned. No other novel of the nineteenth century comes anywhere near *Boadicea* in portraying Mormon society as violent, chaotic, and dysfunctional.

Dime Novel Mormons

Edited and Annotated by Michael Austin and Ardis E. Parshall

Paperback, ISBN: 978-1-58958-566-9

Dime novels probably did more than any other kind of book to turn lower- and middle-class Americans into both book owners and book readers. They were so cheap that almost anyone could afford them, and so exciting that almost everybody wanted to read them. It's hard to tell just how many of these dime novels featured Mormons, but the way Mormons were portrayed in dime novels was remarkably consistent over many decades and multiple genres.

For this volume, four full-length dime novels have been chosen to represent different aspects of the Mormon image in dime novels:

- *Eagle Plume, the White Avenger. A Tale of the Mormon Trail* (1870)
- *The Doomed Dozen; or, Dolores, the Danite's Daughter* (1881)
- *Frank Merriwell Among the Mormons; or, The Lost Tribes of Israel* (1897)
- *The Bradys Among the Mormons; or, Secret Work in Salt Lake City* (1903).

The often-lurid and scandalous portrayals of Mormons in these dime novels had consequences for the relationship between Mormons and the rest of the United States. They would represent reality for millions of people, and the basic portrayals found their way into more serious literature. Understanding how these stereotypes were created and first employed can help us understand many things about the way that Mormonism has always functioned in American culture.

"Swell Suffering": A Biography of Maurine Whipple

Veda Tebbs Hale

Paperback, ISBN: 978-1-58958-124-1
Hardcover, ISBN: 978-1-58958-122-7

Maurine Whipple, author of what some critics consider Mormonism's greatest novel, *The Giant Joshua,* is an enigma. Her prize-winning novel has never been out of print, and its portrayal of the founding of St. George draws on her own family history to produce its unforgettable and candid portrait of plural marriage's challenges. Yet Maurine's life is full of contradictions and unanswered questions. Veda Tebbs Hale, a personal friend of the paradoxical novelist, answers these questions with sympathy and tact, nailing each insight down with thorough research in Whipple's vast but under-utilized collected papers.

Praise for *"Swell Suffering"*:

"Hale achieves an admirable balance of compassion and objectivity toward an author who seemed fated to offend those who offered to love or befriend her. . . . Readers of this biography will be reminded that Whipple was a full peer of such Utah writers as Virginia Sorensen, Fawn Brodie, and Juanita Brooks, all of whom achieved national fame for their literary and historical works during the mid-twentieth century"

—Levi S. Peterson, author of *The Backslider* and *Juanita Brooks: Mormon Historian*

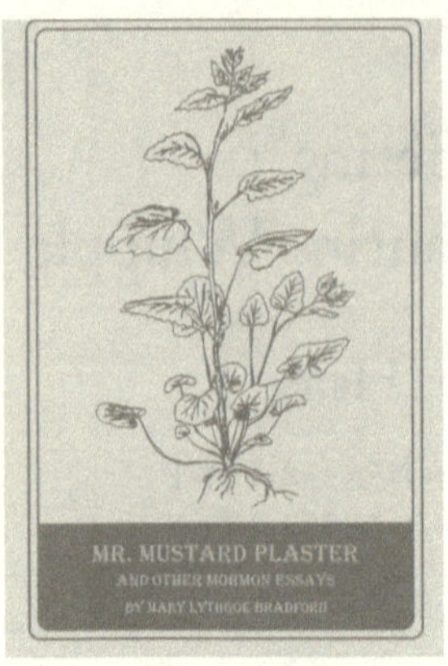

Mr. Mustard Plaster and Other Mormon Essays

Mary Lythgoe Bradford

ISBN: 978-1-58958-742-7

"Mary Bradford is the original literary 'Mormon Girl.' Long before anyone even imagined the bloggernacle, she believed that writing about everyday Mormon life—especially women's lives—could be beautiful and powerful. In her own essays, she brings unparalleled power of perception, generous humanity, and quiet humor to bear on even challenging Mormon subjects. This book is an incredible opportunity for a new generation of Mormon readers to get to know one of our faith's wise women elders. Don't miss it." — Joanna Brooks, author of *The Book of Mormon Girl: A Memoir of an American Faith*

"Mary Bradford believes that the distinctive nature of the personal essay originates from what she calls the three "I's" ("I's," eyes, ayes)—the authors' first-person perspective, their clear and rich vision, and their honest and affirming testimonies of life. Mary's own essays are true to form: her essays are vibrant portraits of a kind and loving soul, a rich and unique perspective, and a life well-lived and deeply loved." — Boyd Jay Petersen, author of *Dead Wood and Rushing Water: Essays on Mormon Faith, Culture, and Family*

"Mary Lythgoe Bradford offers her autobiography in personal essay—revealing a lifetime that bridged generations and pioneered the power of essay in Mormon literature. Since the first issue of Dialogue in 1966, Mary's wisdom and presence as an editor, writer, poet and biographer have linked us together, reaching back to women like Virginia Sorensen and moving us forward into feminism. Today at 84, Mary is still helping 'Mormon women speak.'" — Maxine Hanks, editor of *Women and Authority: Re-emerging Mormon Feminism*

Dead Wood and Rushing Water: Essays on Mormon Faith, Culture, and Family

Boyd Jay Petersen

Paperback, ISBN: 978-1-58958-658-1

For over a decade, Boyd Petersen has been an active voice in Mormon studies and thought. In essays that steer a course between apologetics and criticism, striving for the balance of what Eugene England once called the "radical middle," he explores various aspects of Mormon life and culture—from the Dream Mine near Salem, Utah, to the challenges that Latter-day Saints of the millennial generation face today.

Praise for *Dead Wood and Rushing Water*:

"*Dead Wood and Rushing Water* gives us a reflective, striving, wise soul ruminating on his world. In the tradition of Eugene England, Petersen examines everything in his Mormon life from the gold plates to missions to dream mines to doubt and on to Glenn Beck, Hugh Nibley, and gender. It is a book I had trouble putting down." — Richard L. Bushman, author of *Joseph Smith: Rough Stone Rolling*

"Boyd Petersen is correct when he says that Mormons have a deep hunger for personal stories—at least when they are as thoughtful and well-crafted as the ones he shares in this collection." — Jana Riess, author of *The Twible* and *Flunking Sainthood*

"Boyd Petersen invites us all to ponder anew the verities we hold, sharing in his humility, tentativeness, and cheerful confidence that our paths will converge in the end." — Terryl. L. Givens, author of *People of Paradox: A History of Mormon Culture*

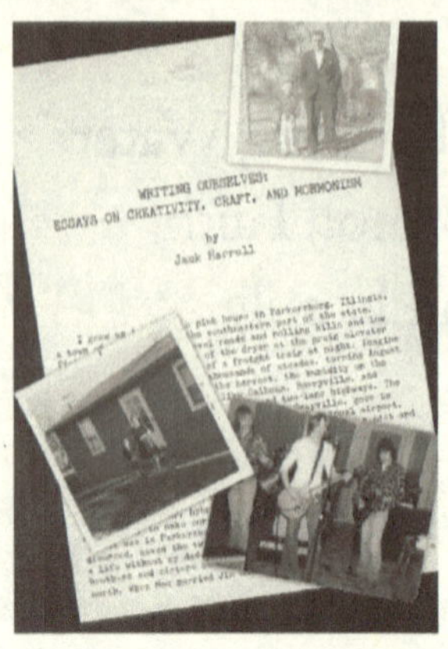

Writing Ourselves: Essays on Creativity, Craft, and Mormonism

Jack Harrell

Paperback, ISBN: 978-1-58958-754-0

Continuing a conversation as old as Mormonism itself, Jack Harrell explores the relationship between Mormonism and the writer. Mormons see the universe in mythic proportions. Their God is a creator, their devil a destroyer. This makes meaningful conflict fundamental to their worldview, and begs the terms for religious redemption, as well as the redemptive power of art. Harrell urges writers to be authentic as they embrace the difficulties inherent in the creative process. His essays blend faithful intellectual inquiry, personal narrative, research, and application to offer insights for anyone who cares about writing, creativity, and the human condition.

Imagining and Reimagining the Restoration

Robert A. Rees

Paperback, ISBN: 978-1-58958-828-8

In *Imagining and Reimagining the Restoration,* Robert A. Rees embarks on an imaginative and profound exploration of Latter-day Saint theology and culture. Through essays, poems, and midrashic interpretations, Rees sheds new light on foundational doctrines, the roles of prophetic imagination, and the divine narratives within the Restoration. He reexamines figures like Joseph Smith and Heavenly Mother, urging readers to embrace a creative and expansive faith perspective that transcends mere tradition.

This captivating work brings readers into a visionary discourse that emphasizes the power of imagination as a spiritual gift. With poetic interludes and scholarly insight, this volume is a transformative invitation to both imagine and reimagine faith, theology, and cultural belonging.

Praise for *Imagining and Reimagining the Restoration*:

"This is a beautiful book, a work of art. Enjoining us to imagine the gospel more deeply, it offers reflections on Christ, Mary, the First Vision, Heavenly Mother, and much else. Robert Rees wants to make us all gospel poets. He also seeks to make us religious critics. He gives his candid views of a broken church in need of mending, commenting on race, women's rights, sexual orientation, and earth stewardship with an imagination turned critical but still filled with warmth and good will. In the end, he invites us to imagine a kindly, loving church blessed with modern sensibilities." — Richard Lyman Bushman, author of *Joseph Smith: Rough Stone Rolling*

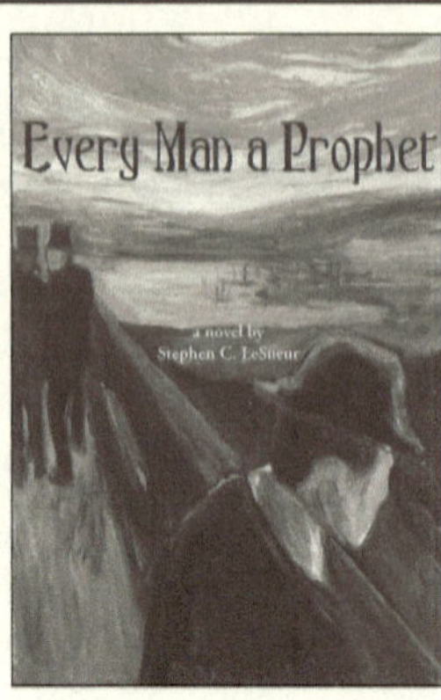

Every Man a Prophet

A Novel by
Stephen C. LeSueur

Paperback, ISBN: 978-1-58958-826-4

Every Man a Prophet by Stephen C. LeSueur is a powerful exploration of faith, love, and self-discovery set within the framework of missionary life in The Church of Jesus Christ of Latter-day Saints. Eddie Pedersen and Orrin Tanner, two missionaries serving in Norway, each grapple with the weight of expectation, personal desires, and the search for their true selves. Eddie struggles to reconcile his faith with feelings he has been taught to suppress, while Orrin's relentless pursuit of perfection masks a deep fear of failure. Together, they navigate a land of cold landscapes and colder hearts, striving to find meaning and connection in their spiritual calling.

Through Eddie and Orrin's intertwined journeys, LeSueur crafts a deeply human story of vulnerability and resilience. The novel delves into the complexities of identity, faith, and the universal longing to belong. As the two men confront the rigid doctrines of their religion and the unyielding truths of their own hearts, readers are drawn into an unforgettable narrative of courage and redemption. *Every Man a Prophet* is a profound tale of the sacrifices we make for faith and the truths we uncover about ourselves along the way..

Praise for *Every Man a Prophet*:

"In *Every Man a Prophet,* not only has Stephen C. LeSueur captured the lives, desires, trials, and struggles of young missionaries and their leaders better than in any other work I have encountered, **he has gifted the world with the best volume of Mormon fiction that I have read.** *Every Man a Prophet* touches hearts, opens minds, and changes lives. . . . It is a book that has the power to touch and change lives and maybe even wards, missions, and the Church." — Andrew Hamilton, Reviews Coordinator, Association for Mormon Letters

www.ingramcontent.com/pod-product-compliance
Lightning Source LLC
LaVergne TN
LVHW050951080826
845145LV00004B/1469

* 9 7 8 1 5 8 9 5 8 8 3 9 4 *